TRUTH AND GRACE MEMORY BOOK

BOOK 2

GRADES 5 - 8

THOMAS K. ASCOL, EDITOR

Published by
Founders Press
Committed to historic Baptist principles
P.O. Box 150931 • Cape Coral, FL 33915
Phone (239) 772-1400 • Fax: (239) 772-1140
Electronic Mail: founders@founders.org or
Website: http://www.founders.org
©2000 Founders Press
Reprinted 2006

Printed in the United States of America

ISBN: 0-9705248-1-1

Unless otherwise indicated, Scripture quotations in this publication are from the New King James Version of the Bible ©1979, 1980, 1984, 1988 Thomas Nelson, Inc., Nashville, TN.

The Shorter Catechism: A Baptist Version is reprinted with permission from Simpson Publishing Company, P.O. Box 100, Avinger, TX 75630

Cover Art by Jonathan Reisinger
Cover Design by Kenneth Puls

Introduction

Dr. Thomas K. Ascol

A Word to Parents

The Bible teaches that children are "a heritage from the Lord" and that "the fruit of the womb is His reward" (Psalm 127:3). Each child is a gift from God. This makes you, as a parent, God's steward. He has entrusted you with one (or more) of His greatest blessings. He has given to you one of His highest callings.

In our day the challenge of parenting has never been greater. Too many moms and dads give in to the temptation to merely "get by." Simply making it through with the fewest possible conflicts becomes the goal. When this attitude is adopted, parents become passive and children learn to be manipulative. One of the saddest, most tragic sights ever to be observed in the Christian Church is a home where parents have defaulted on the responsibilities that God has entrusted to them.

Children are not designed to raise themselves. That is why God gives them parents. Christian parents have been given the specific, gracious duty of raising their children "in the training and admonition of the Lord" (Ephesians 6:4). You cannot be passive and fulfill this responsibility to "bring them up" in the proper way. Prayer, discipline, godly example, and consistent, continuous, clear instruction are the tools that we must employ.

The responsibility to teach children foundational, eternal, life-changing truth from God's Word is laid squarely upon the shoulders of parents by the Lord Himself. Consider the charge that He has given to moms and dads:

> Hear, O Israel: The LORD our God, the LORD is one!
> You shall love the LORD your God with all your heart,

with all your soul, and with all your strength. And these words which I command you today shall be in your heart. You shall teach them diligently to your children, and shall talk of them when you sit in your house, when you walk by the way, when you lie down, and when you rise up (Deuteronomy 6:4–7).

The primary responsibility for teaching your children about God does not belong to the Sunday School or the pastor or any program in the church. God has entrusted this important work to you, dear parent. If you do not invest your time and effort to teach your children about God, be assured that someone else will. The television and theater will teach them that God, if He exists at all, is an irrelevant, indulgent being that is little more than a nice, kindly old man. If you do not teach your children truth and righteousness, be assured that there are a multitude of teachers in this world who would deceive them into thinking that "truth" and morality are relative ideas that can be shaped to fit anyone's beliefs or standards.

Your church stands with you against the false teachers of our age which would destroy the souls of our young people. You have every right to expect that sermons and Sunday School lessons will reinforce the godly principles which you are trying to teach at home. But you have no right to expect the church to take the place of the home. God has given to *parents* the responsibility of teaching their children divine truth.

The *Truth & Grace Memory Book* (TAG) has been designed to help you fulfill this assignment. The emphasis, obviously, is on memorization. Some modern educators have questioned the wisdom of teaching young children to memorize. Concern usually centers on the fear that the child is merely committing to memory meaningless words. This is a real danger—that we will be satisfied with hearing our children merely recite back to us words and sentences about which they have no real understanding. That is why parents must *teach* their children the material in TAG. Personal understanding should always be the goal of our teaching. But understanding will grow (mine has; hasn't yours?). Truth committed to the memory provides the building blocks for such growth.

Discuss the material being memorized with your child. This should be done during the actual memorization as well as at other opportune times in the day. Daily experiences and observations provide a world of opportunities to *illustrate* and *apply* God's Word. For example, the inevitable "night frights" which young children occasionally have, become wonderful occasions to comfortingly remind them that, though we cannot see God, He always sees us. Take time to *define* difficult terms. *Question* your child in order to discover the level of his understanding. When you feel that understanding is being achieved, *pray* with and for the child, including in your prayer some of the concepts just discussed. *Expect* your child to learn, and *rejoice* with him over his growth in knowledge and understanding of God's Word.

No matter what the age of your child, if you will begin immediately, and continue consistently, to teach them with TAG, you will instill in them a comprehensive awareness of the Bible's whole system of revealed truth. Obviously, the earlier a child begins, the better. But TAG has been designed to be useful to young people as well as to children and preschoolers.

Three primary ingredients make TAG a valuable tool in teaching our children God's revealed truth. First and foremost is the Word of God. Several passages have been carefully selected for memorization. Key Bible verses as well as longer portions are designed to introduce children to the overall scope and purpose of God's creative, providential and redemptive activity. The student who completes TAG will read (among other things) the New Testament twice, the 4 Gospels three times, Proverbs five times and the book of Psalms twice. He will memorize (among other texts) the Ten Commandments, the Beatitudes, the Lord's Prayer, 1 Corinthians 13, various psalms (including 119!), plus all the books of the Bible.

Why place such an emphasis on memorizing Scripture? Listen to the Psalmist's answer: "Your word I have hidden in my heart, that I might not sin against You!" (Psalm 119:11). Furthermore, consider the great promise God makes in Isaiah 55:10–11:

> For as the rain comes down, and the snow from heaven,
> and do not return there, but water the earth, and make it

bring forth and bud, that it may give seed to the sower and bread to the eater, so shall My word be that goes forth from My mouth; It shall not return to Me void, but it shall accomplish what I please, and it shall prosper in the thing for which I sent it.

God's Spirit uses the Scripture to speak to adults and children of all ages, calling them to faith in Christ and directing them in the paths of real discipleship. Therefore, as a parent who prays for the salvation and spiritual growth of your child, you must be diligent in teaching him or her the Word of God.

A second element in TAG is a selection of Christian hymns which are to be learned and memorized. Many of these are familiar (such as the Doxology) and can be learned by very small children. Others are not so well-known but are profound in their communication of biblical truth. In all, more than two dozen great hymns of the faith are included.

A third ingredient consists of three different Baptist catechisms, which are spread throughout the three books. The phrase "Baptist catechism" may sound strange to many contemporary Baptists. Some may even consider it to be a contradiction of terms. The truth of the matter, however, is that "catechism" is not a Roman Catholic or Lutheran or Presbyterian word. Rather, it is the anglicized version of the Greek word, *katekeo*, which simply means "to instruct." It appears, in various forms, several times in the Greek New Testament (it is translated as "instructed" in Luke 1:4 and Acts 18:25).

Obviously, then, anyone who has been instructed has in some sense been "catechized." But the word came to refer to a specific type of instruction early in church history. In the early church new Christians were taught the essentials of the faith by learning how to answer specific questions. Certain catechetical questions were grouped together and came to be referred to simply as a "catechism."

From the beginning modern-day Baptists (who emerged in the early 17th century) have employed various catechisms. Catechetical instruction was regarded as a valuable method of teaching both children and adults the doctrinal content of the Bible. Keach's Catechism (whose author, Benjamin Keach—a 17th-century English

Baptist—modeled it after *The Shorter Catechism of the Westminster Assembly*) was widely used among Baptists in both England and America. Charles Spurgeon (19th-century English Baptist leader) revised it slightly and reissued it for use in the Metropolitan Tabernacle. A modern version of this same catechism (*The Shorter Catechism: A Baptist Version*) is introduced in Book 2. A simpler one (*A Catechism for Boys and Girls*) is introduced in Book 1. Tragically, the best known Protestant catechism in the world is largely unknown to most contemporary Baptists. The *Heidelberg Catechism* has been warmly received and widely used since its first German publication in 1563. A 17th-century English Baptist pastor, Hercules Collins, modified this catechism for his congregation and called it the *Orthodox Catechism*. Included in Book 3 is the *Heidelberg Catechism: A Baptist Version* (edited by Tom Ascol).

Southern Baptists of an earlier day freely employed catechisms. One of the first publications which the Sunday School Board produced was a catechism by James Boyce, founder and first President of The Southern Baptist Theological Seminary. John Broadus also wrote a catechism which was published by the board in the 19th century. Lottie Moon used a catechism in her missionary work in China. It is only in recent generations that Southern Baptists have moved away from catechetical instruction as an important tool in teaching God's Word.

By learning a whole, well-constructed catechism a child (or adult for that matter) will be introduced to the overall biblical scheme of salvation. Such discipline will frame the mind for receiving and understanding every part of the Bible. A good catechism helps one to read the Bible theologically.

For these reasons, catechism questions are utilized in TAG. Combined with the other elements, catechetical instruction can prove to be a powerful tool in training our children to be strong in the Lord.

Much hard work has gone into the production of these memory books. Karen Leach and Judy Veilleux have spent long hours in deliberation and refinement in order to see this project completed. We have borrowed ideas from earlier, similar efforts that have been utilized in other churches. Specifically, we built upon an earlier workbook by Paul Settle which was edited for Baptists by Fred Malone and further adapted by Bill Ascol. Rather than further adapt their work, we opted to redesign the idea and come up with a memory book that would more adequately meet the needs of the families of Grace Baptist Church. Now through Founders Press, these TAG books are being made available for wider use. It is with much hope and prayer that homes will be strengthened, children converted and established in the faith, and parents encouraged that this training guide has been produced. May God use it to gain much praise and glory for Himself through our church.

How to Use the Truth and Grace Memory Book

1. Make this memory book something very special in your child's life. Emphasize the importance of learning God's Word. If you are genuinely excited about it, most likely your children will be also.

2. Incorporate it into your regular time of family prayer and devotion. After you have read a portion of God's Word, or some Bible story book, and have prayed, take a few minutes to work on a specific verse or question. Learn to sing the hymns together as a family (You can do it! You simply have to make the effort.).

3. Encourage precise memorization. If they are going to spend the time and effort to learn it, they might as well learn it accurately.

4. Be very positive. Try not to let the memory book become a battleground where a contest of the wills (child's vs. parent's) occurs. This *does not* mean that you let the child dictate when he will or will not work on the material. Rather, do not let yourself get into the position where you are violating biblical principles (by employing rage, sarcasm, ridicule, empty threats, etc.) in your zeal to have your child learn the Bible!

5. Date each step. Throughout TAG there are places for the parent to signify that the student has completed the assignment. Treat each one as a significant milestone and encourage your child to keep progressing.

6. Go at your child's own rate. Children, like adults, learn differently and at different tempos. TAG is designed so that the material can be covered as quickly or slowly as needed. Do not hesitate to move beyond the stated age levels. Remember, these are merely suggestions.

7. Discuss the content of the verses, catechism questions or hymns being learned. Help your child understand what they are saying. Remember, the goal is spiritual understanding, *not* mechanical regurgitation.

8. Review. Avoid placing such an emphasis on advancement that your child is tempted to utilize only his or her short-term rather than long-term memory.

9. Rejoice. Your child is learning Bible truths that some adults will never know. Thank the Lord for the privilege of teaching your children about Him. Be encouraged as you hear them reciting the Word of God and expressing important biblical truths.

10. Pray. Ask God to drive His Word deep into the heart and conscience of each child. Pray that He will send His Spirit to teach them inwardly the truth about sin and judgment, heaven and hell, Jesus and salvation. As you diligently teach your children, labor in prayer for them until you see Christ being formed in them.

11. Encourage other parents. We all need it. Make a conscious effort to give it. Training our children in the way of the Lord is a high calling. We are constantly tempted to neglect it. We all fail at some point and at some time. Resolve to be an encourager.

OUTLINE

The following is an outline of memory work from Book 2 divided into suggested age/grade levels. If you are not beginning with 5th grade, we suggest that you begin with the appropriate Scripture, hymns, etc. for your child, as well as with question #1 of *The Shorter Catechism: A Baptist Version*. The catechism is written in a systematic format with each question built upon those before it. The memorization of the whole catechism will expose the child to a solid doctrinal foundation.

5th Grade

6th Grade

7th Grade

8th Grade

5th Grade

Psalm 103:1–8

    Bless the LORD, O my soul;
    And all that is within me, bless His holy name!
    Bless the LORD, O my soul,
    And forget not all His benefits:
    Who forgives all your iniquities,
    Who heals all your diseases,
    Who redeems your life from destruction,
    Who crowns you with lovingkindness and tender mercies,
    Who satisfies your mouth with good things,
    So that your youth is renewed like the eagle's.

    The LORD executes righteousness
    And justice for all who are oppressed.
    He made known His ways to Moses,
    His acts to the children of Israel.
    The LORD is merciful and gracious,
    Slow to anger, and abounding in mercy.

Date: _____

Isaiah 46:9–10

    Remember the former things of old,
    For I am God, and there is no other;
    I am God, and there is none like Me,
    Declaring the end from the beginning,
    And from ancient times things that are not yet done,
    Saying, "My counsel shall stand,
    And I will do all My pleasure."

Date: _____

Deuteronomy 29:29

The secret things belong to the LORD our God, but those things which are revealed belong to us and to our children forever, that we may do all the words of this law.

Date: _____

Ephesians 1:2–9

Grace to you and peace from God our Father and the Lord Jesus Christ. Blessed be the God and Father of our Lord Jesus Christ, who has blessed us with every spiritual blessing in the heavenly places in Christ, just as He chose us in Him before the foundation of the world, that we should be holy and without blame before Him in love, having predestined us to adoption as sons by Jesus Christ to Himself, according to the good pleasure of His will, to the praise of the glory of His grace, by which He has made us accepted in the Beloved. In Him we have redemption through His blood, the forgiveness of sins, according to the riches of His grace which He made to abound toward us in all wisdom and prudence, having made known to us the mystery of His will, according to His good pleasure which He purposed in Himself.

Date: _____

Proverbs 6:16–19

These six things the LORD hates,
Yes, seven are an abomination to Him: A proud look,
A lying tongue,
Hands that shed innocent blood,
A heart that devises wicked plans,
Feet that are swift in running to evil,
A false witness who speaks lies,
And one who sows discord among brethren.

Date: _____

Proverbs 18:24

A man who has friends must himself be friendly,
But there is a friend who sticks closer than a brother.

Date: _____

Hebrews 11:6

But without faith it is impossible to please Him, for he who
comes to God must believe that He is, and that He is a rewarder
of those who diligently seek Him.

Date: _____

Psalm 119:41–56

Let Your mercies come also to me, O LORD—
Your salvation according to Your word.
So shall I have an answer for him who reproaches me,
For I trust in Your word.
And take not the word of truth utterly out of my mouth,
For I have hoped in Your ordinances.
So shall I keep Your law continually,
Forever and ever.
And I will walk at liberty,
For I seek Your precepts.
I will speak of Your testimonies also before kings,
And will not be ashamed.
And I will delight myself in Your commandments,
Which I love.
My hands also I will lift up to Your commandments,
Which I love,
And I will meditate on Your statutes.

Remember the word to Your servant,
Upon which You have caused me to hope.

This is my comfort in my affliction,
For Your word has given me life.
The proud have me in great derision,
Yet I do not turn aside from Your law.
I remembered Your judgments of old, O LORD,
And have comforted myself.
Indignation has taken hold of me
Because of the wicked, who forsake Your law.
Your statutes have been my songs
In the house of my pilgrimage.
I remember Your name in the night, O LORD,
And I keep Your law.
This has become mine,
Because I kept Your precepts.

Date: _____

Exodus 20:1–17 (The Ten Commandments):
And God spoke all these words, saying:
"I am the LORD your God, who brought you out of the land of Egypt, out of the house of bondage.

You shall have no other gods before Me.

You shall not make for yourself a carved image, or any likeness of anything that is in heaven above, or that is in the earth beneath, or that is in the water under the earth; you shall not bow down to them nor serve them. For I, the LORD your God, am a jealous God, visiting the iniquity of the fathers on the children to the third and fourth generations of those who hate Me, but showing mercy to thousands, to those who love Me and keep My commandments.

You shall not take the name of the LORD your God in vain, for the LORD will not hold him guiltless who takes His name in vain.

Remember the Sabbath day, to keep it holy. Six days you shall labor and do all your work, but the seventh day is the Sabbath of the LORD your God. In it you shall do no work: you, nor your son, nor your daughter, nor your male servant, nor your female servant, nor your cattle, nor your stranger who is within your gates. For in six days the LORD made the heavens and the earth, the sea, and all that is in them, and rested the seventh day. Therefore the LORD blessed the Sabbath day and hallowed it.

Honor your father and your mother, that your days may be long upon the land which the LORD your God is giving you.

You shall not murder.

You shall not commit adultery.

You shall not steal.

You shall not bear false witness against your neighbor.

You shall not covet your neighbor's house; you shall not covet your neighbor's wife, nor his male servant, nor his female servant, nor his ox, nor his donkey, nor anything that is your neighbor's."

Date: _____

Hymn: *The Church's One Foundation*

The church's one foundation
Is Jesus Christ her Lord;
She is His new creation,
By Spirit and the Word:
From heaven He came and sought her
To be His holy bride,
With His own blood He bought her,
And for her life He died.

Elect from every nation,
Yet one o'er all the earth,
Her charter of salvation,
One Lord, one faith, one birth;
One holy name she blesses,
Partakes one holy food,
And to one hope she presses,
With every grace endued.

'Mid toil and tribulation,
And tumult of her war,
She waits the consummation
Of peace forevermore;
Till with the vision glorious,
Her longing eyes are blest,
And the great church victorious
Shall be the church at rest.

Yet she on earth hath union
With God the Three and One,
And mystic sweet communion
With those whose rest is won:
O happy ones and holy!
Lord, give us grace that we,
Like them, the meek and lowly,
On high may dwell with Thee.

Amen.

Words by Samuel J. Stone (1866)

Date: _____

Hymn: *When I Survey the Wondrous Cross*

When I survey the wondrous cross,
On which the Prince of glory died,
My richest gain I count but loss,
And pour contempt on all my pride.

Forbid it, Lord, that I should boast,
Save in the death of Christ my God;
All the vain things that charm me most,
I sacrifice them to His blood.

See, from His head, His hands, His feet
Sorrow and love flow mingled down;
Did e'er such love and sorrow meet,
Or thorns compose so rich a crown.

Were the whole realm of nature mine,
That were a present far to small;
Love so amazing, so divine,
Demands my soul, my life, my all.

Amen.

Words by Isaac Watts (1707)

Date: _____

Mid-Year Review by Teacher_____
Year-End Review by Teacher_____

6th Grade

John 14:1–7

"Let not your heart be troubled; you believe in God, believe also in Me. In My Father's house are many mansions; if it were not so, I would have told you. I go to prepare a place for you. And if I go and prepare a place for you, I will come again and receive you to Myself; that where I am, there you may be also. And where I go you know, and the way you know." Thomas said to Him, "Lord, we do not know where You are going, and how can we know the way?" Jesus said to him, "I am the way, the truth, and the life. No one comes to the Father except through Me. If you had known Me, you would have known My Father also; and from now on you know Him and have seen Him."

Date: _____

Matthew 22:36–40

"Teacher, which is the great commandment in the law?" Jesus said to him, "You shall love the LORD your God with all your heart, with all your soul, and with all your mind. This is the first and great commandment. And the second is like it: You shall love your neighbor as yourself. On these two commandments hang all the Law and the Prophets."

Date: _____

Mark 10:45

For even the Son of Man did not come to be served, but to serve, and to give His life a ransom for many.

Date: _____

1 Corinthians 13

Though I speak with the tongues of men and of angels, but have not love, I have become sounding brass or a clanging cymbal. And though I have the gift of prophecy, and understand all mysteries and all knowledge, and though I have all faith, so that I could remove mountains, but have not love, I am nothing. And though I bestow all my goods to feed the poor, and though I give my body to be burned, but have not love, it profits me nothing. Love suffers long and is kind; love does not envy; love does not parade itself, is not puffed up; does not behave rudely, does not seek its own, is not provoked, thinks no evil; does not rejoice in iniquity, but rejoices in the truth; bears all things, believes all things, hopes all things, endures all things. Love never fails. But whether there are prophecies, they will fail; whether there are tongues, they will cease; whether there is knowledge, it will vanish away. For we know in part and we prophesy in part. But when that which is perfect has come, then that which is in part will be done away. When I was a child, I spoke as a child, I understood as a child, I thought as a child; but when I became a man, I put away childish things. For now we see in a mirror, dimly, but then face to face. Now I know in part, but then I shall know just as I also am known. And now abide faith, hope, love, these three; but the greatest of these is love.

Date: _____

Ecclesiastes 12:13–14

Let us hear the conclusion of the whole matter:
Fear God and keep His commandments, for this is the whole duty of man. For God will bring every work into judgment, including every secret thing, whether it is good or whether it is evil.

Date: _____

Psalm 119:57–80

You are my portion, O LORD;
I have said that I would keep Your words.
I entreated Your favor with [my] whole heart;
Be merciful to me according to Your word.
I thought about my ways,
And turned my feet to Your testimonies.
I made haste, and did not delay
To keep Your commandments.
The cords of the wicked have bound me,
But I have not forgotten Your law.
At midnight I will rise to give thanks to You,
Because of Your righteous judgments.
I am a companion of all who fear You,
And of those who keep Your precepts.
The earth, O LORD, is full of Your mercy;
Teach me Your statutes.
You have dealt well with Your servant,
O LORD, according to Your word.
Teach me good judgment and knowledge,
For I believe Your commandments.
Before I was afflicted I went astray,
But now I keep Your word.
You are good, and do good;
Teach me Your statutes.
The proud have forged a lie against me,
But I will keep Your precepts with my whole heart.
Their heart is as fat as grease,
But I delight in Your law.
It is good for me that I have been afflicted,
That I may learn Your statutes.
The law of Your mouth is better to me
Than thousands of coins of gold and silver.

Your hands have made me and fashioned me;
Give me understanding, that I may learn Your commandments.
Those who fear You will be glad when they see me,
Because I have hoped in Your word.
I know, O LORD, that Your judgments are right,
And that in faithfulness You have afflicted me.
Let, I pray, Your merciful kindness be for my comfort,
According to Your word to Your servant.
Let Your tender mercies come to me, that I may live;
For Your law is my delight.
Let the proud be ashamed,
For they treated me wrongfully with falsehood;
But I will meditate on Your precepts.
Let those who fear You turn to me,
Those who know Your testimonies.
Let my heart be blameless regarding Your statutes,
That I may not be ashamed.

Date: _____

The Apostles' Creed

I believe in God the Father Almighty,
Maker of the heavens and earth.

And in Jesus Christ His only begotten Son, our Lord,
Who was conceived by the Holy Spirit,
Born of the Virgin Mary,
Suffered under Pontius Pilate,
Was crucified, dead and buried;
The third day He rose again from the dead:
He ascended into heaven,
And sits on the right hand of God the Father Almighty;
From there He shall come to judge the living and the dead.

I believe in the Holy Spirit,
The holy catholic church,
The communion of saints,
The forgiveness of sins,
The resurrection of the body
And the life everlasting.
Amen.

(NOTE: The meaning of "catholic" is not to be confused with the Roman Catholic Church. It means universal.)

Date: _____

Hymn: *How Sweet and Awful Is the Place*

How sweet and awful is the place
With Christ within the doors,
While everlasting love displays
The choicest of her stores.

While all our hearts and all our songs
Join to admire the feast,
Each of us cry, with thankful tongues,
"Lord, why was I a guest?"

"Why was I made to hear Thy voice
And enter while there's room,
When thousands make a wretched choice,
And rather starve than come?"

'Twas the same love that spread the feast
That sweetly drew us in;
Else we had still refused to taste,
And perished in our sin.

Pity the nations, O our God,
Constrain the earth to come;
Send Thy victorious Word abroad,
And bring the strangers home.

We long to see Thy churches full,
That all the chosen race
May, with one voice and heart and soul,
Sing thy redeeming grace.

Amen.

Words by Isaac Watts (1707)

Date: _____

Hymn: *Hallelujah, Praise Jehovah*

Hallelujah, praise Jehovah,
O my soul, Jehovah praise;
I will sing the glorious praises
Of my God through all my days.
Put no confidence in princes,
Nor for help on man depend;
He shall die, to dust returning,
And his purposes shall end.

Happy is the man that chooses
Israel's God to be his aid;
He is blessed whose hope of blessing
On the Lord his God is stayed.
Heav'n and earth the Lord created,
Seas and all that they contain;
He delivers from oppression,
Righteousness He will maintain.

Food He daily gives the hungry,
Sets the mourning pris'ner free,
Raises those bowed down in anguish,
Makes the sightless eyes to see.
Well Jehovah loves the righteous,
And the stranger He befriends,
Helps the fatherless and widow,
Judgment on the wicked sends.

Hallelujah, praise Jehovah,
O my soul, Jehovah praise;
I will sing the glorious praises
Of my God through all my days.
Over all God reigns forever,
Though all ages He is King;
Unto Him, thy God, O Zion,
Joyful hallelujahs sing.

Amen.

From Psalm 146 in *The Psalter* (1912)

Date: _____

Read:

Proverbs   Date: _____

John   Date: _____

1 John   Date: _____

Mid-Year Review by Teacher: _____
Year-End Review by Teacher: _____

7th Grade

John 15:16

You did not choose Me, but I chose you and appointed you that you should go and bear fruit, and that your fruit should remain, that whatever you ask the Father in My name He may give you.

Date: _____

John 17:9–11

I pray for them. I do not pray for the world but for those whom You have given Me, for they are Yours. And all Mine are Yours, and Yours are Mine, and I am glorified in them. Now I am no longer in the world, but these are in the world, and I come to You. Holy Father, keep through Your name those whom You have given Me, that they may be one as We are.

Date: _____

Romans 8:29–30

For whom He foreknew, He also predestined to be conformed to the image of His Son, that He might be the firstborn among many brethren. Moreover whom He predestined, these He also called; whom He called, these He also justified; and whom He justified, these He also glorified.

Date: _____

Proverbs 21:23

Whoever guards his mouth and tongue
Keeps his soul from troubles.

Date: _____

Proverbs 16:32

He who is slow to anger is better than the mighty,
And he who rules his spirit than he who takes a city.

Date: _____

Proverbs 23:23

Buy the truth, and do not sell it,
Also wisdom and instruction and understanding.

Date: _____

Psalm 27

The LORD is my light and my salvation;
Whom shall I fear?
The LORD is the strength of my life;
Of whom shall I be afraid?
When the wicked came against me
To eat up my flesh,
My enemies and foes,
They stumbled and fell.
Though an army may encamp against me,
My heart shall not fear;
Though war should rise against me,
In this I will be confident.

One thing I have desired of the LORD,
That will I seek:
That I may dwell in the house of the LORD
All the days of my life,
To behold the beauty of the LORD,
And to inquire in His temple.
For in the time of trouble
He shall hide me in His pavilion;

In the secret place of His tabernacle
He shall hide me;
He shall set me high upon a rock.

And now my head shall be lifted up
Above my enemies all around me;
Therefore I will offer sacrifices of joy in His tabernacle;
I will sing, yes, I will sing praises to the LORD.
Hear, O LORD, when I cry with my voice!
Have mercy also upon me, and answer me.
When You said, "Seek My face,"

My heart said to You, "Your face, LORD, I will seek."
Do not hide Your face from me;
Do not turn Your servant away in anger;
You have been my help;
Do not leave me nor forsake me,
O God of my salvation.
When my father and my mother forsake me,
Then the LORD will take care of me.

Teach me Your way, O LORD,
And lead me in a smooth path, because of my enemies.
Do not deliver me to the will of my adversaries;
For false witnesses have risen against me,
And such as breathe out violence.
I would have lost heart, unless I had believed
That I would see the goodness of the LORD
In the land of the living.
Wait on the LORD;
Be of good courage,
And He shall strengthen your heart;
Wait, I say, on the LORD!

Date: _____

Psalm 119:81–112

My soul faints for Your salvation,
But I hope in Your word.
My eyes fail from searching Your word, Saying,
"When will You comfort me?"
For I have become like a wineskin in smoke,
Yet I do not forget Your statutes.
How many are the days of Your servant?
When will You execute judgment on those who persecute me?
The proud have dug pits for me,
Which is not according to Your law.
All Your commandments are faithful;
They persecute me wrongfully;
Help me!
They almost made an end of me on earth,
But I did not forsake Your precepts.
Revive me according to Your lovingkindness,
So that I may keep the testimony of Your mouth.

Forever, O LORD,
Your word is settled in heaven.
Your faithfulness endures to all generations;
You established the earth, and it abides.
They continue this day according to Your ordinances,
For all are Your servants.
Unless Your law had been my delight,
I would then have perished in my affliction.
I will never forget Your precepts,
For by them You have given me life.
I am Yours, save me;
For I have sought Your precepts.
The wicked wait for me to destroy me,
But I will consider Your testimonies.
I have seen the consummation of all perfection,
But Your commandment is exceedingly broad.

Oh, how I love Your law!
It is my meditation all the day.
You, through Your commandments, make me wiser than my enemies;
For they are ever with me.
I have more understanding than all my teachers,
For Your testimonies are my meditation.
I understand more than the ancients,
Because I keep Your precepts.
I have restrained my feet from every evil way,
That I may keep Your word.
I have not departed from Your judgments,
For You Yourself have taught me.
How sweet are Your words to my taste,
Sweeter than honey to my mouth!
Through Your precepts I get understanding;
Therefore I hate every false way.

Your word is a lamp to my feet
And a light to my path.
I have sworn and confirmed
That I will keep Your righteous judgments.
I am afflicted very much;
Revive me, O LORD, according to Your word.
Accept, I pray, the freewill offerings of my mouth, O LORD,
And teach me Your judgments.
My life is continually in my hand,
Yet I do not forget Your law.
The wicked have laid a snare for me,
Yet I have not strayed from Your precepts.
Your testimonies I have taken as a heritage forever,
For they are the rejoicing of my heart.
I have inclined my heart to perform Your statutes
Forever, to the very end.

Date: _____

Read:

Matthew	Date: _____
Mark	Date: _____
Luke	Date: _____
John	Date: _____

Hymn: *Great is Thy Faithfulness*

Great is Thy faithfulness, O God my Father,
There is no shadow of turning with Thee;
Thou changest not, Thy compassions, they fail not;
As Thou hast been Thou forever wilt be.

> Refrain:
> Great is Thy faithfulness!
> Great is Thy faithfulness!
> Morning by morning new mercies I see;
> All I have needed Thy hand hath provided;
> Great is Thy faithfulness, Lord, unto me!

Summer and winter, and springtime and harvest,
Sun, moon and stars in their courses above
Join with all nature in manifold witness
To Thy great faithfulness, mercy and love.

(Refrain)

Pardon for sin and a peace that endureth,
Thine own dear presence to cheer and to guide;

Strength for today and bright hope for tomorrow,
Blessings all mine, with ten thousand beside!

(Refrain)

Amen.

Words by Thomas O. Chisholm (1923)

Date: _____

Hymn: *Come Ye Sinners*

Come, ye sinners, poor and wretched,
Weak and wounded, sick and sore;
Jesus ready stands to save you,
Full of pity joined with pow'r:
    He is able,
    He is able,
    He is able,
He is willing; doubt no more.

Come, ye needy, come and welcome,
God's free bounty glorify;
True belief and true repentance,
Ev'ry grace that brings you nigh,
    Without money,
    Without money,
    Without money,
Come to Jesus Christ and buy.

Come, ye weary, heavy laden,
Bruised and broken by the fall;
If you tarry till you're better,
You will never come at all:
    Not the righteous,
    Not the righteous,
    Not the righteous—
Sinners Jesus came to call.

Let not conscience make you linger,
Nor of fitness fondly dream;
All the fitness he requireth
Is to feel your need of Him;
    This He gives you,
    This He gives you,
    This He gives you;
'Tis the Spirit's rising beam.

Lo! th' incarnate God ascended,
Pleads the merit of His blood;
Ventures on Him, venture wholly,
Let no other trust intrude:
    None but Jesus,
    None but Jesus,
    None but Jesus
Can do helpless sinners good.

Amen.

Words by Joseph Hart (1759)

Date: _____

Mid-Year Review by Teacher: _____
Year-End Review by Teacher: _____

8th Grade

Philippians 2:5–13
Let this mind be in you which was also in Christ Jesus, who, being in the form of God, did not consider it robbery to be equal with God, but made Himself of no reputation, taking the form of a bondservant, and coming in the likeness of men. And being found in appearance as a man, He humbled Himself and became obedient to the point of death, even the death of the cross. Therefore God also has highly exalted Him and given Him the name which is above every name, that at the name of Jesus every knee should bow, of those in heaven, and of those on earth, and of those under the earth, and that every tongue should confess that Jesus Christ is Lord, to the glory of God the Father. Therefore, my beloved, as you have always obeyed, not as in my presence only, but now much more in my absence, work out your own salvation with fear and trembling; for it is God who works in you both to will and to do for His good pleasure.

Date: _____

Galatians 2:16
Knowing that a man is not justified by the works of the law but by faith in Jesus Christ, even we have believed in Christ Jesus, that we might be justified by faith in Christ and not by the works of the law; for by the works of the law no flesh shall be justified.

Date: _____

Ephesians 2:8–10

For by grace you have been saved through faith, and that not of yourselves; it is the gift of God, not of works, lest anyone should boast. For we are His workmanship, created in Christ Jesus for good works, which God prepared beforehand that we should walk in them.

Date: _____

2 Corinthians 12:9

And He said to me, "My grace is sufficient for you, for My strength is made perfect in weakness." Therefore most gladly I will rather boast in my infirmities, that the power of Christ may rest upon me.

Date: _____

Isaiah 26:3–4

You will keep him in perfect peace,
Whose mind is stayed on You,
Because he trusts in You.
Trust in the LORD forever,
For in YAH, the LORD, is everlasting strength.

Date: _____

Proverbs 15:5

A fool despises his father's instruction,
But he who receives reproof is prudent.

Date: _____

Psalm 119:113–136

I hate the double-minded,
But I love Your law.
You are my hiding place and my shield;
I hope in Your word.
Depart from me, you evildoers,
For I will keep the commandments of my God!
Uphold me according to Your word, that I may live;
And do not let me be ashamed of my hope.
Hold me up, and I shall be safe,
And I shall observe Your statutes continually.
You reject all those who stray from Your statutes,
For their deceit is falsehood.
You put away all the wicked of the earth like dross;
Therefore I love Your testimonies.
My flesh trembles for fear of You,
And I am afraid of Your judgments.

I have done justice and righteousness;
Do not leave me to my oppressors.
Be surety for Your servant for good;
Do not let the proud oppress me.
My eyes fail from seeking Your salvation
And Your righteous word.
Deal with Your servant according to Your mercy,
And teach me Your statutes.
I am Your servant;
Give me understanding,
That I may know Your testimonies.
It is time for You to act, O LORD,
For they have regarded Your law as void.
Therefore I love Your commandments
More than gold, yes, than fine gold!
Therefore all Your precepts concerning all things
I consider to be right;
I hate every false way.

Your testimonies are wonderful;
Therefore my soul keeps them.
The entrance of Your words gives light;
It gives understanding to the simple.
I opened my mouth and panted,
For I longed for Your commandments.
Look upon me and be merciful to me,
As Your custom is toward those who love Your name.
Direct my steps by Your word,
And let no iniquity have dominion over me.
Redeem me from the oppression of man,
That I may keep Your precepts.
Make Your face shine upon Your servant,
And teach me Your statutes.
Rivers of water run down from my eyes,
Because men do not keep Your law.

Date: _____

Isaiah 55:6–11

Seek the LORD while He may be found,
Call upon Him while He is near.
Let the wicked forsake his way,
And the unrighteous man his thoughts;
Let him return to the LORD,
And He will have mercy on him;
And to our God,
For He will abundantly pardon.

"For My thoughts are not your thoughts,
Nor are your ways My ways," says the LORD.
"For as the heavens are higher than the earth,
So are My ways higher than your ways,
And My thoughts than your thoughts.

For as the rain comes down, and the snow from heaven,
And do not return there,
But water the earth,
And make it bring forth and bud,
That it may give seed to the sower
And bread to the eater,
So shall My word be that goes forth from My mouth;
It shall not return to Me void,
But it shall accomplish what I please,
And it shall prosper in the thing for which I sent it."

Date: _____

Read:

Acts	Date: _____
Romans	Date: _____
1 Corinthians	Date: _____
2 Corinthians	Date: _____
Proverbs	Date: _____

Hymn: *A Mighty Fortress Is Our God*

A mighty fortress is our God,
A bulwark never failing;
Our helper He, amid the flood
Of mortal ills prevailing:
For still our ancient foe
Doth seek to work us woe;
His craft and power are great,
And armed with cruel hate,
On earth is not his equal.

Did we in our own strength confide,
Our striving would be losing;
Were not the right Man on our side,
The Man of God's own choosing:
Dost ask who that may be?
Christ Jesus it is He;
Lord Sabbaoth, His name,
From age to age the same,
And He must win the battle.

And tho' this world, with devils filled,
Should threaten to undo us,
We will not fear, for God hath willed
His truth to triumph through us:
The Prince of Darkness grim—
We tremble not for him;
His rage we can endure,
For lo, his doom is sure,
One little word shall fell him.

That word above all earthly powers,
No thanks to them, abideth;
The Spirit and the gifts are ours
Thro' Him who with us sideth:
Let goods and kindred go,
This mortal life also;
The body they may kill:
God's truth abideth still,
His kingdom is forever.

Amen.

Words by Martin Luther (1529)
From Psalm 46

Date: _____

Hymn: *Stand Up, Stand Up For Jesus*

Stand up, stand up for Jesus,
Ye soldiers of the cross;
Lift high the royal banner,
It must not suffer loss:
From vict'ry unto vict'ry
His army shall He lead,
Till ev'ry foe is vanquished,
And Christ is Lord indeed.

Stand up, Stand up for Jesus,
Stand in His strength alone;
The arm of flesh will fail you,
Ye dare not trust your own:

Put on the gospel armor,
Each piece put on with prayer;
Where duty calls or danger,
Be never wanting there.

Stand up, stand up for Jesus,
The strife will not be long;
This day the noise of battle,
The next the victor's song:
To him that overcometh
A crown of life shall be;
He, with the King of glory,
Shall reign eternally.

Amen.

Words by George Duffield (1858)

Date: _____

Mid-Year Review by Teacher: _____
Year-End Review by Teacher: _____

The Shorter Catechism: A Baptist Version

1. **What is the chief end of man?**
   Man's chief end is to glorify God, and to enjoy Him forever.

   (Psalm 73:25–28; Romans 11:36; 1 Corinthians 10:31)

   Date: _____

2. **What rule has God given to direct us how we may glorify and enjoy Him?**
   The word of God, namely the Scriptures of the Old and New Testaments, is the only rule to direct us how we may glorify and enjoy Him.

   (Luke 16:29, 31; Galatians 1:8–9; Ephesians 2:20; 2 Timothy 3:15–16; 1 John 1:3–4)

   Date: _____

3. **Are the Scriptures trustworthy in all that they affirm?**
   The Scriptures of both the Old and New Testaments, being God-breathed, are infallible and inerrant in all their parts and are, therefore, trustworthy in all that they affirm concerning history, science, doctrine, ethics, religious practice, or any other topic.

   (John 10:35; 1 Thessalonians 2:13; 2 Timothy 3:16)

   Date: _____

4. **What do the Scriptures principally teach?**
The Scriptures principally teach what man is to believe concerning God, and what duty God requires of man.

(Micah 6:8; 2 Timothy 1:13; 3:16)

Date: _____

5. **What is God?**
God is a Spirit, infinite, eternal, and unchangeable, in His being, wisdom, power, holiness, justice, goodness and truth.

(Exodus 3:14; 34:6–7; Job 11:7–9; 42:2; Psalm 90:2; 147:5; John 4:24; James 1:17; Revelation 4:8; 15:4)

Date: _____

6. **Are there more Gods than one?**
There is but one only, the living and true God.

(Deuteronomy 6:4; Jeremiah 10:10)

Date: _____

7. **How many persons are there in the Godhead?**
There are three persons in the Godhead: the Father, Son and the Holy Spirit; and these three are one God, the same in substance, equal in power and glory.

(Matthew 28:19; John 10:30; Acts 5:3–4; 2 Corinthians 13:14)

Date: _____

8. **What are the decrees of God?**
The decrees of God are His eternal purpose, according to the counsel of His will, whereby, for His own glory, He has foreordained whatsoever comes to pass.

(Daniel 4:35; Romans 11:36; Ephesians 1:4, 11–12)

Date: _____

9. **How does God execute His decrees?**
God executes His decrees in the works of creation and providence.

(Ephesians 1:11; Revelation 4:11)

Date: _____

10. **What is the work of creation?**
The work of creation is God's making all things of nothing, by the word of His power, in the space of six days, and all very good.

(Genesis 1:1–31; Exodus 20:11; Colossians 1:16; Hebrews 11:3)

Date: _____

11. **How did God create man?**
God created man, male and female, after His own image, in knowledge, righteousness and holiness, with dominion over the creatures.

(Genesis 1:26–28; Ecclesiastes 7:29; Ephesians 4:24; Colossians 3:10)

Date: _____

12. **What are God's works of providence?**
God's works of providence are His most holy, wise and powerful preserving and governing all His creatures, and all their actions.

(Psalm 103:19; 104:24; 145:17; Isaiah 28:29; Matthew 10:29–31; Colossians 1:17; Hebrews 1:3)

Date: _____

13. **What was the estate wherein man was created?**

Man was created in an estate of sinlessness and happiness in which the Lord God entrusted him with care for the garden of Eden and forbade him to eat from the tree of the knowledge of good and evil, upon the pain of death.

(Genesis 1:31; 2:7–9, 15–17, 25; Ecclesiastes 7:29)

Date: _____

14. **Did our first parents continue in the estate wherein they were created?**

Our first parents, being left to the freedom of their own will, fell from the estate wherein they were created, by sinning against God.

(Genesis 3:6–8, 13, 17; Ecclesiastes 7:29)

Date: _____

15. **What is sin?**

Sin is any lack of conformity unto, or transgression of, the law of God.

(1 John 3:4)

Date: _____

16. **What was the sin whereby our first parents fell from the estate wherein they were created?**

The sin whereby our first parents fell from the estate wherein they were created, was their eating the forbidden fruit.

(Genesis 3:6, 9–13)

Date: _____

17. Did all mankind fall in Adam's first transgression?

Because the prohibition regarding the forbidden fruit was given to Adam as a representative of mankind, he disobeyed not only for himself, but for his posterity; so that all mankind, descending from Adam by ordinary generation, sinned in him and fell with him in his first transgression.

(Genesis 2:16–17; Romans 5:12, 18–19; 1 Corinthians 15:21–22)

Date: _____

18. Into what estate did the fall bring mankind?

The fall brought mankind into an estate of sin and misery.

(Genesis 3:16–19; Romans 5:12)

Date: _____

19. Wherein consists the sinfulness of that estate whereinto man fell?

The sinfulness of that estate whereinto man fell, consists in the guilt of Adam's first sin, the lack of original righteousness and the corruption of his whole nature, which is commonly called original sin; together with all actual transgressions which proceed from it.

(Psalm 51:5; Ecclesiastes 7:29; Matthew 15:19–20; Romans 3:10; 5:12, 19; Ephesians 2:1–3; James 1:14–15)

Date: _____

20. What is the misery of that estate whereinto mankind fell?

All mankind by their fall lost communion with God, are under His wrath and curse, and so made liable to all miseries in this life, to death itself and to the pains of hell forever.

(Genesis 3:8, 10, 24; Lamentations 3:39; Matthew 25:41, 46; Romans 6:23; Ephesians 2:2–3)

Date: _____

21. **Did God leave all mankind to perish in the estate of sin and misery?**

God having, out of His mere good pleasure, from all eternity, elected some to everlasting life, did establish a way of salvation, to deliver them out of the estate of sin and misery, and to bring them into an estate of salvation by a Redeemer.

(Acts 13:48; Romans 3:20–22; Galatians 3:21–22; Ephesians 1:4)

Date: _____

22. **Who is the Redeemer of God's elect?**

The only Redeemer of God's elect is the Lord Jesus Christ, who being the eternal Son of God became man, and so was, and continues to be, God and man, in two distinct natures, and one person forever.

(Luke 1:35; John 1:14; Romans 9:5; Galatians 4:4; Colossians 2:9; 1 Timothy 2:5–6; Hebrews 7:24–25)

Date: _____

23. **How did Christ, being the Son of God, become man?**

Christ, the Son of God, became man, by taking to Himself a true body and a reasonable soul, being conceived by the power of the Holy Spirit, in the womb of the Virgin Mary, and born of her, yet without sin.

(Matthew 26:38; Luke 1:27, 31, 35, 42; Galatians 4:4; Hebrews 2:14; 4:15; 7:26)

Date: _____

24. What offices does Christ execute as the Redeemer?
Christ, as the Redeemer, executes the offices of a Prophet, Priest and of a King, both in His estate of humiliation and exaltation.

(Psalm 2:6; Isaiah 9:6–7; Matthew 21:5; Acts 3:21–22; Hebrews 5:5–7; 7:25)

Date: _____

25. How does Christ execute the office of a prophet?
Christ executes the office of a prophet in revealing to His people, by His Word and Spirit, the will of God for their salvation.

(John 1:18; 14:26; 20:31; 1 Peter 1:10–12)

Date: _____

26. How does Christ execute the office of a priest?
Christ executes the office of a priest, in His once offering up of Himself a sacrifice for the sins of His people to satisfy divine justice, and to reconcile them to God, and making continual intercession for them.

(Romans 5:10; Hebrews 2:17; 7:24–25; 9:14, 28)

Date: _____

27. How does Christ execute the office of a king?
Christ executes the office of a king in calling His church out of the world to be a people for Himself, and in ruling and defending it; subduing, saving, preserving and blessing His elect; and in restraining, conquering and taking vengeance on all His and their enemies.

(Psalm 110:2–3; Isaiah 32:1–2; 33:22; 63:9; Matthew 16:18; Acts 5:31; 15:14–16; 1 Corinthians 15:25; Ephesians 1:22; 4:11–12; 2 Thessalonians 1:8–9; 1 Peter 2:9–10; Revelation 2:10; 22:12)

Date: _____

28. **Wherein did Christ's humiliation consist?**

Christ's humiliation consisted in His being born, and that in a low condition, made under the law, undergoing the miseries of this life, the wrath of God and the cursed death of the cross; in being buried and continuing under the power of death for a time.

(Isaiah 53:2–3; Matthew 27:46; Luke 2:7; 22:44; Acts 2:24–27, 31; 1 Corinthians 15:3–4; Galatians 4:4; Philippians 2:8; Hebrews 12:2–3)

Date: _____

29. **Wherein consists Christ's exaltation?**

Christ's exaltation consists in His rising again from the dead on the third day, in ascending up into heaven, in sitting at the right hand of God the Father, and in coming to judge the world at the last day.

(Mark 16:19; Acts 1:9–11; 17:31; 1 Corinthians 15:4; Ephesians 1:20–21)

Date: _____

30. **How are God's elect made partakers of the redemption purchased by Christ?**

God's elect are made partakers of the redemption purchased by Christ, by God the Father's effectual application of it to them by His Holy Spirit.

(John 1:11–12; Romans 8:29; Titus 3:5–6)

Date: _____

31. **How does the Father by the Spirit apply to His elect the redemption purchased by Christ?**

The Father by the Spirit applies to His elect the redemption purchased by Christ, by working faith in them, and uniting them to Christ in their effectual calling.

(John 1:12–13; 3:5; 6:37, 39, 44; 1 Corinthians 1:9; Ephesians 2:8; Philippians 1:29)

Date: _____

32. What is effectual calling?

Effectual calling is the work of God the Father's power and grace, whereby He, by His Word and Spirit, invites and draws His elect unto Jesus Christ; convincing them of their sin and misery, enlightening their minds in the knowledge of Christ, and renewing their wills, thereby persuading and enabling them to embrace Jesus Christ, freely offered to all in the gospel.

(Deuteronomy 30:6; Psalm 110:3; Ezekiel 36:26–27; Matthew 11:25–28; 16:16–17; John 1:12–13; 3:5; 6:44–45, 63; 16:8–11; Acts 26:18; Romans 8:29–30; 1 Corinthians 1:9; Philippians 2:13; 2 Thessalonians 2:13–14; 2 Timothy 1:8–9; James 1:18; 1 Peter 1:23, 25)

Date: _____

33. What benefits do they that are effectually called partake of in this life?

They that are effectually called do in this life partake of justification, adoption and sanctification, and the several benefits which in this life, do either accompany or flow from them.

(Romans 8:30; 1 Corinthians 1:26, 30; 6:11; Ephesians 1:5)

Date: _____

34. What is justification?

Justification is an act of God's free grace unto sinners effectually called to Jesus Christ, wherein He pardons all their sins, and accepts them as righteous in His sight, only for the righteousness of Christ imputed to them, and received by faith alone.

(Romans 3:24–25; 4:6–8; 5:17–19; 8:30; 2 Corinthians 5:19, 21; Galatians 2:16; Philippians 3:9)

Date: _____

35. What is adoption?

Adoption is an act of God's free grace, whereby all those who are justified are received into the number, and have a right to all the privileges of the sons of God.

(John 1:12; Romans 8:17; 1 John 3:1)

Date: _____

36. What is sanctification?

Sanctification is the work of God's free grace, whereby His elect are renewed in the whole man after the image of God, and are enabled more and more to die unto sin and live unto righteousness.

(Romans 6:4–6; 8:1; Galatians 5:24; Ephesians 4:23–24; Philippians 1:6; 2:12–13; 2 Thessalonians 2:13; 1 John 5:4)

Date: _____

37. What are the benefits which in this life do accompany or flow from justification, adoption and sanctification?

The benefits which in this life do accompany or flow from justification, adoption and sanctification are assurance of God's love, peace of conscience, joy in the Holy Spirit, increase of grace and perseverance therein to the end.

(Proverbs 4:18; Romans 5:1–2, 5; 14:17; 1 Peter 1:5)

Date: _____

38. What benefits do believers receive from Christ at death?

The souls of believers are, at their death, made perfect in holiness, and do immediately pass into glory; and their bodies, being still united to Christ, do rest in their graves until the resurrection.

(Job 19:26–27; Isaiah 57:2; Luke 23:43; 2 Corinthians 5:1, 6, 8; Philippians 1:23; 1 Thessalonians 4:14, 16; Hebrews 12:23)

Date: _____

39. What shall be done to the wicked at their death?

The souls of the wicked are, at their death, cast into the torments of hell, and their bodies lie in their graves until the resurrection and judgment of the great day.

(Luke 16:23–24; John 5:28–29; Acts 24:15; 2 Peter 2:9)

Date: _____

40. What benefits do believers receive from Christ at the resurrection?

At the resurrection, believers being raised up in glory, shall be openly acknowledged and acquitted in the day of judgment, and made perfectly blessed in the full enjoyment of God to all eternity.

(Matthew 10:32; 25:23; 1 Corinthians 13:12; 15:42–43; Philippians 3:21; 1 Thessalonians 4:17–18; 1 John 3:2)

Date: _____

41. What shall be done to the wicked at the day of judgment?

At the day of judgment, the wicked being raised to dishonor, shall be sentenced to the unspeakable torments of body and soul in hell with the devil and his angels for all eternity.

(Daniel 12:2; Matthew 13:49–50; 25:41, 46; John 5:28–29; 2 Thessalonians 1:8–9; Revelation 14:10–11)

Date: _____

42. What is the duty which God requires of man?

The duty which God requires of man is obedience to His revealed will.

(Ecclesiastes 12:13–14; Micah 6:8)

Date: _____

43. **What did God at first reveal to man for the rule of his obedience?**
The rule which God at first revealed to man for his obedience was the moral law.

(Romans 2:14:15)

Date: _____

44. **Where is the moral law summarily comprehended?**
The moral law is summarily comprehended in the Ten Commandments.

(Deuteronomy 10:4; Matthew 19:17)

Date: _____

45. **What is the sum of the Ten Commandments?**
The sum of the Ten Commandments is, to love the Lord our God with all our hearts, with all our soul, with all our strength and with all our mind; and our neighbor as ourselves.

(Matthew 22:37–40)

Date: _____

46. **What is the preface to the Ten Commandments?**
The preface to the Ten Commandments is in these words, "I am the LORD your God, who brought you out of the land of Egypt, out of the house of bondage."

(Exodus 20:2)

Date: _____

47. **What does the preface to the Ten Commandments teach us?**

The preface to the Ten Commandments teaches us that because God is the LORD, and our God and Redeemer, therefore we are bound to keep all His commandments.

(Deuteronomy 11:1; Psalm 100:2–3; Jeremiah 10:7; Luke 1:74–75)

Date: _____

48. **What is the first commandment?**

The first commandment is, "You shall have no other gods before Me."

(Exodus 20:3)

Date: _____

49. **What is required in the first commandment?**

The first commandment requires us to know and acknowledge God to be the only true God, and our God; and to worship and glorify Him accordingly.

(Deuteronomy 26:17; 1 Chronicles 28:9; Psalm 29:2; Matthew 4:10)

Date: _____

50. **What is forbidden in the first commandment?**

The first commandment forbids the denying, or not worshipping and glorifying the true God as God, and our God; and the giving of that worship and glory to any other which is due to Him alone.

(Psalm 14:1; 81:10–11; Romans 1:20–21, 25–26)

Date: _____

51. **What are we specially taught by the words "before Me" in the first commandment?**

The words "before Me" in the first commandment teach us that God—who sees all things—takes notice of, and is much displeased with, the sin of having any other god.

(Psalm 44:20–21)

Date: _____

52. **What is the second commandment?**

The second commandment is, "You shall not make for yourself a carved image, or any likeness of anything that is in heaven above, or that is in the earth beneath, or that is in the water under the earth; you shall not bow down to them nor serve them. For I, the LORD your God, am a jealous God, visiting the iniquity of the fathers on the children to the third and fourth generations of those who hate Me, but showing mercy to thousands, to those who love Me and keep My commandments."

(Exodus 20:4–6)

Date: _____

53. **What is required in the second commandment?**

The second commandment requires the receiving, observing and keeping pure and entire, all such religious worship and ordinances as God has appointed in His Word.

(Deuteronomy 12:13–14, 32; 32:46; Matthew 28:20; Mark 7:6–8; John 4:24; Acts 2:42)

Date: _____

54. What is forbidden in the second commandment?

The second commandment forbids the worshipping of God by images, or any other way not appointed in His Word.

(Leviticus 10:1–2; Deuteronomy 4:15–19; 12:30–32)

Date: _____

55. What are the reasons annexed to the second commandment?

The reasons annexed to the second commandment are, God's sovereignty over us, His ownership of us and the zeal He has to His own worship.

(Exodus 34:13–14; Psalm 95:2–3, 6; 100:2–3; 106:19, 21, 23)

Date: _____

56. What is the third commandment?

The third commandment is, "You shall not take the name of the LORD your God in vain, for the LORD will not hold him guiltless who takes His name in vain."

(Exodus 20:7)

Date: _____

57. What is required in the third commandment?

The third commandment requires the holy and reverent use of God's names, titles attributes, ordinances, Word and works.

(Psalm 29:2; 105:1–5; 138:1–2; Ecclesiastes 5:1; Malachi 1:11, 14; Matthew 6:9; Revelation 15:3–4)

Date: _____

58. What is forbidden in the third commandment?
The third commandment forbids all profaning or abusing of any thing whereby God makes Himself known.

(Malachi 1:6–7, 12; 2:2; 3:14)

Date: _____

59. What is the reason annexed to the third commandment?
The reason annexed to the third commandment is, that however the breakers of this commandment may escape punishment from men, yet the Lord our God will not permit them to escape His righteous judgment.

(Deuteronomy 28:58–59; 1 Samuel 2:12, 17, 22, 29; 3:13; Malachi 2:2)

Date: _____

60. What is the fourth commandment?
The fourth commandment is, "Remember the Sabbath day, to keep it holy. Six days you shall labor and do all your work, but the seventh day is the Sabbath of the LORD your God. In it you shall do no work: you, nor your son, nor your daughter, nor your male servant, nor your female servant, nor your cattle nor your stranger who is within your gates. For in six days the LORD made the heavens and the earth, the sea and all that is in them, and rested the seventh day. Therefore the LORD blessed the Sabbath day and hallowed it."
(Exodus 20:8–11)

Date: _____

61. What is required in the fourth commandment?
The fourth commandment requires the keeping holy to God such set times as He has appointed in His Word; expressly one whole day in seven is to be a holy Sabbath to Himself.

(Leviticus 19:30; Deuteronomy 5:12–14)

Date: _____

62. **Which day of the seven has God appointed to be the weekly Sabbath?**

From the beginning of the world to the resurrection of Christ, God appointed the seventh day of the week to be the weekly Sabbath; and the first day of the week ever since, to continue to the end of the world, which is the Christian Sabbath.

(Genesis 2:2–3; Acts 20:7; 1 Corinthians 16:1–2; Revelation 1:10)

Date: _____

63. **How is the Sabbath to be sanctified?**

The Sabbath is to be sanctified by a holy resting all that day, even from worldly employments and recreations as are lawful on the other days; and spending the whole time in the public and private exercises of God's worship, except so much as is to be taken up in the works of necessity and mercy.

(Exodus 16:25–28; 20:8, 10; Leviticus 23:3; Nehemiah 13:15–22; Psalm 92:1–2; Isaiah 66:23; Matthew 12:11–12; Luke 4:16; Acts 20:7)

Date: _____

64. **What is forbidden in the fourth commandment?**

The fourth commandment forbids the omission or careless performance of the duties required, and the profaning of the day by idleness, or doing that which is in itself sinful, or by unnecessary thoughts, words or works, about our worldly employments of recreations.

(Isaiah 58:13; Jeremiah 17:24–26; Ezekiel 22:26; 23:38; Amos 8:5; Malachi 1:13)

Date: _____

65. What are the reasons annexed to the fourth commandment?

The reasons annexed to the fourth commandment are God's allowing us six days of the week for our own employments, His claiming a special right to the seventh, His own example and His blessing the Sabbath day.

(Genesis 2:3; Exodus 20:9–10, 12; 31:15–17; Leviticus 23:3)

Date: _____

66. What is the fifth commandment?

The fifth commandment is, "Honor your father and your mother, that your days may be long upon the land which the LORD your God is giving you."

(Exodus 20:12)

Date: _____

67. What is required in the fifth commandment?

The fifth commandment requires the preserving the honor of, and performing the duties belonging to, every one in their several places and relations, as superiors, inferiors or equals.

(Romans 12:10; 13:1; Ephesians 5:21–23; 6:1–2, 5, 9; 1 Peter 2:13–14, 17)

Date: _____

68. What is forbidden in the fifth commandment?

The fifth commandment forbids the neglecting of, or doing anything against, the honor and duty which belongs to every one in their several places and relations.

(Ezekiel 34:2; Matthew 15:4–6; Romans 13:7–8)

Date: _____

69. What is the reason annexed to the fifth commandment?
The reason annexed to the fifth commandment is a promise of long life and prosperity (as far as it shall serve for God's glory and their own good) to all such as keep this commandment.

(Deuteronomy 5:16; Ephesians 6:2–3)

Date: _____

70. What is the sixth commandment?
The sixth commandment is, "You shall not murder."

(Exodus 20:13)

Date: _____

71. What is required in the sixth commandment?
The sixth commandment requires all lawful endeavors to preserve our own life, and the life of others.

(1 Kings 18:4; Job 29:13; Psalm 82:3–4; Ephesians 5:28–29)

Date: _____

72. What is forbidden in the sixth commandment?
The sixth commandment forbids the taking away of our own life, or the life of our neighbor unjustly, or whatsoever tends thereunto.

(Genesis 9:6; Leviticus 19:17; Proverbs 24:11–12; Acts 16:28)

Date: _____

73. What is the seventh commandment?
The seventh commandment is, "You shall not commit adultery."

(Exodus 20:14)

Date: _____

74. **What is required in the seventh commandment?**
The seventh commandment requires the preservation of our own and our neighbor's chastity, in heart, speech and behavior.

(1 Corinthians 7:2; Ephesians 5:4, 11–12; 1 Thessalonians 4:3–5; 2 Timothy 2:22; 1 Peter 3:2)

Date: _____

75. **What is forbidden in the seventh commandment?**
The seventh commandment forbids all unchaste thoughts, words and actions.

(Matthew 5:28; 15:19; Ephesians 5:3–4)

Date: _____

76. **What is the eighth commandment?**
The eighth commandment is, "You shall not steal."

(Exodus 20:15)

Date: _____

77. **What is required in the eighth commandment?**
The eighth commandment requires the lawful procuring and furthering the wealth and outward estate of ourselves and others.

(Exodus 23:4– 5; Leviticus 25:35; Deuteronomy 22:1–4; Job 29:11–17; Proverbs 27:23; Acts 20:33–35; Philippians 2:4; 1 Timothy 5:8)

Date: _____

78. **What is forbidden in the eighth commandment?**
The eighth commandment forbids whatsoever does, or may, unjustly hinder our own, or our neighbor's, wealth or outward estate.

(Proverbs 21:17; 23:20–21; 28:19; Ephesians 4:28)

Date: _____

79. **What is the ninth commandment?**
The ninth commandment is, "You shall not bear false witness against your neighbor."

(Exodus 20:16)

Date: _____

80. **What is required in the ninth commandment?**
The ninth commandment requires the maintaining and promoting of truth between man and man, and of our own and our neighbor's good name, especially in witness-bearing.

(Proverbs 14:5, 25: Zechariah 8:16; Acts 25:10; 1 Peter 3:16; 3 John 12)

Date: _____

81. **What is forbidden in the ninth commandment?**
The ninth commandment forbids whatsoever is prejudicial to truth, or injurious to our own or our neighbor's good name.

(Leviticus 19:16; Job 27:5; Psalm 15:3; Romans 3:13)

Date: _____

82. What is the tenth commandment?

The tenth commandment is, "You shall not covet your neighbor's house; you shall not covet your neighbor's wife, nor his manservant, nor his maidservant, nor his ox, nor his donkey, nor anything that is your neighbor's."

(Exodus 20:17)

Date: _____

83. What is required in the tenth commandment?

The tenth commandment requires full contentment with our own condition, with a right and charitable frame of spirit toward our neighbor, and all that is his.

(Job 31:29–30; Romans 12:15; 1 Corinthians 13:4–7; 1 Timothy 1:5; 6:6; Hebrews 13:5)

Date: _____

84. What is forbidden in the tenth commandment?

The tenth commandment forbids all discontent with our estate, envying of grieving at the good if our neighbor, and all inordinate motions and affections to anything that is his.

(1 Kings 21:4; Esther 5:13; 1 Corinthians 10:10; Galatians 5:26; Colossians 3:5; James 3:14, 16)

Date: _____

85. Is any man able perfectly to keep the commandments of God?

No mere man since the fall is able, in this life, perfectly to keep the commandments of God; but daily breaks them in thought, word and deed.

(Genesis 6:5; 8:21; Ecclesiastes 7:20; Romans 3:9–20; Galatians 5:17; James 3:2–12; 1 John 1:8, 10)

Date: _____

86. **Are all transgressions of the law equally heinous?**
Some sins in themselves, and by reason of several aggravations, are more heinous in the sight of God than others.

(Ezekiel 8:6, 13, 15; John 19:11)

Date: _____

87. **What does every sin deserve?**
Every sin deserves God's wrath and curse, both in this life and that which is to come.

(Lamentations 3:39; Matthew 25:41; Galatians 3:10; Ephesians 5:6)

Date: _____

88. **What way of escape has God revealed to sinners that they may be saved from His wrath and curse due to them for their sin?**
God has revealed to sinners the gospel of His Son, Jesus Christ, as the only way of salvation from their sins.

(Acts 4:12; Romans 1:16)

Date: _____

89. **What does God, in His gospel, require of sinners that they may be saved?**
God, in His gospel, requires of sinners faith in Jesus Christ and repentance unto life that they may escape His wrath due for their sin, and be saved.

(Acts 20:21)

Date: _____

90. **What is faith in Jesus Christ?**
Faith in Jesus Christ is a saving grace, whereby sinners receive and rest upon Him alone for salvation, as He is offered to them in the gospel.

(John 1:12; Romans 10:14,17; Galatians 2:16; Ephesians 2:8–9; Philippians 3:9)

Date: _____

91. **What is repentance unto life?**
Repentance unto life is a saving grace, whereby a sinner, out of a true sense of his sin, and apprehension of the mercy of God in Christ, does, with grief and hatred of his sin, turn from it unto God, with full purpose of, and endeavor after, new obedience.

(Psalm 119:59; Jeremiah 31:18–19; Ezekiel 36:31; Joel 2:12–13; Acts 2:37–38; 11:18)

Date: _____

92. **Will all who outwardly profess obedience to the gospel escape the wrath due for their sins?**
Not all who outwardly profess obedience to the gospel, but only those who persevere in faith and holiness to the end shall be saved.

(Matthew 7:21; Hebrews 12:14; 1 Peter 1:5)

Date: _____

93. **Who then will persevere in faith and holiness unto the end and be saved?**

All true believers, by reason of God's eternal decree and unchangeable love, Christ's intercession and the Spirit and Word of God abiding in them, are preserved by the power of God and supplied with every spiritual blessing in Christ, and therefore will most certainly persevere in faith and holiness unto the end and be saved.

(Jeremiah 31:3; John 10:28–29; 14:16; Romans 8:28–30; 1 Corinthians 1:8–9; Ephesians 1:3; Philippians 1:6; Hebrews 7:25; 1 Peter 1:5)

Date: _____

94. **What are the outward and ordinary means of grace whereby God preserves his elect and communicates to them the blessings of redemption in Christ?**

The outward and ordinary means of grace whereby God preserves his elect and communicates to them the blessings of redemption in Christ are his ordinances, especially the Word, the sacraments and prayer; all which are made effectual to the elect for salvation.

(Matthew 28:19–20; Acts 2:41–42, 46–47)

Date: _____

95. **How is the Word made effectual to salvation?**

The Spirit of God makes the reading, but especially the preaching of the Word, an effectual means of convincing and converting sinners and of building up believers in holiness and comfort through faith unto salvation.

(Nehemiah 8:8; Psalm 19:7–8; Acts 20:32; Romans 1:16; 10:13–17; 15:4; 1 Corinthians 1:21; 14:24–25; 1 Thessalonians 1:6; 1 Timothy 4:13, 16; 2 Timothy 3:15–17)

Date: _____

96. **How is the Word to be read and heard, that it may become effectual to salvation?**

That the Word may become effectual to salvation, the hearers of the Word must attend thereunto with diligence, preparation and prayer; receive it with faith and love, lay it up in their hearts, and practice it in their lives.

(Psalm 119:11, 18; Proverbs 8:34; Luke 8:15; 2 Thessalonians 2:10; Hebrews 4:2; James 1:25; 1 Peter 2:1–2)

Date: _____

97. **What is a sacrament of the new covenant?**

A sacrament of the new covenant is a holy ritual instituted by Jesus Christ; wherein, by sensible signs, Christ and the benefits of the new covenant are represented, sealed and applied to believers.

(1 Corinthians 11:23–26)

Date: _____

98. **What are the sacraments of the new covenant?**

The sacraments of the new covenant are baptism and the Lord's supper.

(Matthew 28:19; 1 Corinthians 11:23–26)

Date: _____

99. **How do baptism and the Lord's supper become effectual means of salvation?**

Baptism and the Lord's supper become effectual means of salvation, not from any virtue in them, or in him that administers them; but only by the blessing of Christ, and the working of His Spirit in those who by faith receive them.

(1 Corinthians 3:6–7; 1 Peter 3:21)

Date: _____

100. What is baptism?

Baptism is a sacrament of the new covenant instituted by Jesus Christ, to be unto the person baptized a sign of his fellowship with Him, in His death, burial and resurrection; of his being ingrafted into Him; of remission of sins; and of his giving up himself unto God through Jesus Christ, to live and walk in newness of life.

(Matthew 28:19; Romans 6:3–4; Galatians 3:26–27; Colossians 2:12)

Date: _____

101. To whom is baptism to be administered?

Baptism is to be administered to all those who credibly profess repentance towards God, faith in and obedience to our Lord Jesus Christ and to none other.

(Mark 16:16; Acts 2:38, 41; 8:12)

Date: _____

102. Are the infants of professing believers to be baptized?

The infants of professing believers are not to be baptized, because there is neither command nor example in the Holy Scriptures, nor certain inference from them, to baptize such.

(Deuteronomy 12:32; Proverbs 30:6; Acts 8:12; 10:47–48)

Date: _____

103. How is baptism rightly administered?

Baptism is rightly administered by immersion, or dipping the whole body of the believer in water, in the name of the Father, and of the Son and the Holy Spirit, according to Christ's institution, and the practice of the apostles, and not by sprinkling or pouring of water, or dipping some part of the body, after the tradition of men.

(Matthew 3:16; John 3:23; Acts 8:38–39)

Date: _____

104. What is the Lord's supper?

The Lord's supper is a sacrament of the new covenant, wherein, by giving and receiving bread and fruit of the vine, according to Christ's appointment, His death is shown forth; and the worthy receivers are, not after a corporal and carnal manner, but by faith, made partakers of His body and blood, with all His benefits, to their spiritual nourishment and growth in grace.

(1 Corinthians 10:16; 11:23–26)

Date: _____

105. What is required for the worthy receiving of the Lord's supper?

It is required of them that would worthily partake of the Lord's supper, that they examine themselves of their knowledge to discern the Lord's body, of their faith to feed upon Him, of their repentance, love and new obedience; lest coming unworthily, they eat and drink judgement to themselves.

(1 Corinthians 5:7–8; 11:16–17, 28–29, 31; 2 Corinthians 13:5)

Date: _____

106. What is prayer which is acceptable to God?

Acceptable prayer is an offering up of the desires of the righteous unto God, for things agreeable to His will, in the name of Christ, by the help of His Spirit, with confession of sins, and thankful acknowledgement of His mercies.

(Psalm 32:5–6; 62:8; Proverbs 15:8; 28:9; Daniel 9:4; John 16:23; Romans 8:26; Philippians 4:6; 1 John 5:14)

Date: _____

107. **What rule has God given for the direction of His people in prayer?**

The whole Word of God is of use to direct His people in prayer, but the special rule of direction is that pattern of prayer which Christ taught His disciples, commonly called *The Lord's Prayer.*

(Matthew 6:9–13; Luke 11:2–4; 1 John 5:14)

Date: _____

108. **What does the preface of the Lord's prayer teach His disciples?**

The preface of the Lord's prayer (which is "Our Father in heaven") teaches His disciples, commonly called Christians, to draw near to God with all holy reverence and confidence, as children to a father, able and ready to help them; and that they should pray with and for others.

(Isaiah 64:9; Matthew 6:9; Luke 11:13; Acts 11:26; Romans 8:15; Ephesians 6:18; 1 Timothy 2:1–2)

Date: _____

109. **What do Christians pray for in the first petition?**

In the first petition (which is, "Hallowed be Your name") Christians pray that God would enable them and others to glorify Him in all that whereby He makes Himself known, and that He would dispose all things to His own glory.

(Psalms 67:1–3; Matthew 6:9; Romans 11:36)

Date: _____

110. What do Christians pray for in the second petition?

In the second petition (which is, "Your kingdom come") Christians pray that Satan's kingdom may be destroyed, and that the kingdom of grace may be advanced, sinners brought into it, and believers kept in it, and that the kingdom of glory may be hastened.

(Psalm 51:18, 68:1; Matthew 6:10; Romans 10:1; Colossians 1:9–13; 2 Thessalonians 3:1; Revelation 12:10–11; 22:20)

Date: _____

111. What do Christians pray for in the third petition?

In the third petition (which is, "Your will be done on earth as it is in heaven.") Christians pray that God by His grace would make them able and willing to know, obey and submit to His will in all things, as the angels do in heaven.

(Job 1:21; Psalms 103:20–21; 119:34–36; Matthew 6:10; Acts 21:14)

Date: _____

112. What do Christians pray for in the fourth petition?

In the fourth petition (which is, "Give us this day our daily bread.") Christians pray that of God's free gift they may receive a competent portion of the good things of this life, and enjoy His blessing with them.

(Psalm 90:17; Proverbs 30:8–9; Matthew 6:11; 1 Timothy 4:4–5)

Date: _____

113. What do Christians pray for in the fifth petition?

In the fifth petition (which is, "And forgive us our debts, as we forgive our debtors") Christians pray that God, for Christ's sake, would freely pardon all their sins; which they are the more readily encouraged to ask, because by His grace they are enabled from the heart to forgive others.

(Psalm 51:1–2, 7, 9; Daniel 9:17–19; Matthew 6:12; 18:35; Luke 11:4)

Date: _____

114. What do Christians pray for in the sixth petition?

In the sixth petition (which is, "And do not lead us into temptation, but deliver us from the evil one") Christians pray that God would either keep them from being tempted to sin, or support and deliver them when they are tempted.

(Psalm 19:13; 51:10, 12; Matthew 6:13; 26:41)

Date: _____

115. What does the conclusion of the Lord's prayer teach His disciples?

The conclusion of the Lord's prayer (which is, "For Yours is the kingdom and the power and the glory forever. Amen") teaches His disciples to take their encouragement in prayer from God only, and in their prayers to praise Him; ascribing kingdom, power and glory to Him; and in testimony of their desire and assurance to be heard, to say, Amen.

(1 Chronicles 29:10–13; Daniel 9:4,7–9, 16–19; Matthew 6:13; 1 Corinthians 14:16; Revelation 4:11; 22:20)

Date: _____